Old Wolf's
Search for Pinocchio

Reading Practice with Ellie's Code

Level **4**

By

ELIANA VILLARROEL

Illustrated by

Nicole Yang

Ellie's Code

Text and illustrations copyright ©2013 by Eliana Villarroel

ISBN 978-0-9911507-4-8

The research-based method used in Ellie's Code is designed to teach children and older non-readers, including those with reading difficulties, learning disabilities, and English language learners, to decode and build fluency.

Color-coded words aid and guide the brain to identify silent letters, recognize and focus on mini-words within words and spelling patterns, to process faster. This develops automaticity leading to greater fluency.

Using this color-coded method allows the reader to discover a unique, simple method to decode the English language with ease and enjoyment.

For eight years, this method was thoroughly tested and successfully used with hundreds of special education students, English language learners, and students who were identified at risk because of their inability to read and write at grade level.

After approximately 30 hours of instruction, the average reading fluency growth had an increase of 39 words per minute. Grade level reading fluency tests with black text were used to determine progress. All participants came from first through fifth grade levels. Students who participated in the program were first identified as being far below basic or below basic in reading fluency. Students made an easy transition from the color-coded material to all black text.

Young and older readers with or without disabilities or reading difficulties can enjoy this story and benefit from the code. This level 4 book is recommended for students in the sixth grade and beyond.

Ellie's Code

SUMMARY GUIDE FOR COLOR-CODE USAGE:

COLOR CODE:	USE:	SAMPLES:
BLUE LETTER (S)	• Identify whole words or mini-words within word(s) and/or spelling patterns that can be easily decoded in isolation.	**as, fast, has, all, call, can, the, them, for, only, just, think, story, together, watch, you, before**
GREEN LETTER (S)	• Complete all the sounds required to decode the word when added to the blue letters and/or the blue and red letters.	**they, was, about, maybe, words, ants**
	• May serve to identify the change of nouns from singular to plural.	**legs, pigs, bricks**
	• Regular verb-tense endings: (present progressive, past tense)	**doing, falling, saying, looked, called**
	• Adverb endings as needed.	**luckily, proudly**

RED LETTER (S)	• Identify silent letter(s). Important to remember for spelling.	one, why, know, watch, school, answered
	• May alert the reader to change the previous vowel(s) sound from a short vowel to a long vowel, or vice versa.	time, made, like, give, have
	• Guides the reader to focus on decoding the blue short/long vowel while ignoring the red vowel for vowel digraphs (two successive letters whose phonetic value is a single sound).	your, yours, could, please, people, thought, because
	• Help to distinguish the correct meaning of a homophone (Two or more words pronounced alike but are different in meaning, derivation or spelling.)	to, too, two right, write their, there hear, here

I dedicate this story to the loving memory of
my great-aunt *Maria Pegottini*,
my grandmother *Transito Pegottini-Blatch*,
my mother *Nelly Blatch-Villarroel*
and
my father *Carlos Villarroel-Soriano*.
You will remain in my heart until the end of time.

I also wish to dedicate this story to all
of my special education students and to
the *Schurr High School RTI tutors*
who did an awesome job.
I want to give special recognition to my editor
and great friend *Patricia Tongate*.
I thank you for your fabulous work.

♣

This story began the morning when Old Wolf left Green Valley to help Gepetto find his beloved Pinocchio. He tried not to get sentimental about his departure. Deep inside, however, he knew he would miss his new friends just as much as he still missed the Little Red Hen and her family. After wiping his tears and blowing his nose, Old Wolf tried to regain his composure and focus on his last venture.

The Old Wolf had been warned that the path to the coast was a bit treacherous. He knew he had to hurry if he was to find a ship that would take him to the Italian port of Tuscany. Old Wolf had never been on a ship before and the whole idea of trying something new was exciting. With great enthusiasm, he quickly programmed his GPS watch to guide him on his journey to the coast.

It was around noon when Old Wolf decided to rest under an old cypress tree and eat some of the food which Jack's mother had packed for him. Suddenly, he heard soft footsteps crushing the dead leaves behind the tree. "Who goes there?" asked Old Wolf somewhat apprehensively.

"It is me, Knip Tibbar! I was told that you plan to cross the Amethyst Valley on your way to the coast," answered a fearless voice coming from an elegantly dressed pink rabbit.

"That is true! But how do you know about my plans?" asked Old Wolf.

"Oh, dear Mr. Old Wolf! When you have lived as long as I and still have your lucky rabbit's foot attached to your body, the rest is plain. Your plan is to plot a plausible path to get safely to the coast without being plundered or plucked. As a rabbit with plenty of practice, it will be my pleasure to offer you plenty of advice.

"You see, in order to reach Amethyst Valley which you can view from this great plateau, you must have a plan. This is not the time for playtime or pleasantry. Since you appear to be a pleasant Old Wolf with good intentions to help those less fortunate, you need not plead with or placate me. Time should not be wasted because time will **not** wait for you!" declared Knip Tibbar.

"Mr. Tibbar, you are indeed an eloquent rabbit and although you almost confused me, I think I understand your idea. Please tell me, where did you learn to speak that way and why is your name so unusual?" asked the Old Wolf.

"You see Old Wolf, when I was a bunny I was sent to a special school. I had trouble learning to read and write words because my mind visualized letters and numbers in reverse. I would write my name backward and, as a result, everyone called me 'Knip Tibbar.' I actually liked the way my name sounded in reverse, so it did not bother me. Thank God the teacher was nice and stopped the others from making fun of me, especially when I stuttered. She told my mother that I had a brilliant mind just that my brain was wired a bit differently. She suggested that I learn to compensate by closing my eyes "to get out of the mirror's trap." To this day, there are times when my brain works like it is still trapped inside a mirror. Now when I get excited, instead of stuttering and mispronouncing the sound of the letter "r" or confusing it with the sound of the letter "l", my brain has learned to adjust by providing me with other suitable words which begin with a "pr-" or "pl-". This way, others will focus on my message and not on my flaws, as it should always be!" clarified Mr. Knip Tibbar.

"What a splendid strategy, Mr. Tibbar! I also had trouble in school. How I wish I had stayed in school to learn how to read and write. Looking back, I realize that I chose the easy way out. Maybe someday I can still learn," replied the wistful Old Wolf.

"It's only too late when you have given up! You decide what to do with time. Otherwise, time is not kind to those who do not put forth effort and try! Wishes and yearnings only create fleeting and vanishing fantasies," challenged Knip Tibbar.

"Now, we must hurry to get you across the Amethyst Valley. It is a beautiful valley covered with lavender flowers. Be warned, however, if you linger and cannot find your way out, the fragrance of the flowers will make you relax. You will forget about time. Eventually, the fragrance will put you to sleep and you may never, ever wake up!

"I will give you two useful gifts which you should never keep in the same pocket. A mirror which looks beyond the present time and a pocket watch which reads time backwards to remind you that time is precious. You must keep them with you at all times to stay focused on your present task.

"However, to be fully protected, you must find the four-leaf clover which is hidden and guarded by the purple pansies in the middle of the lavender field. The only way anyone ever gets out of this valley is with the protection of the four-leaf clover, which the pansies hide. These flowers are very delicate and timid, so you must speak softly to them and say the following chant:

Pretty precious purple pansies

please disclose the four-leaf clover

to provide me with

the privilege of a probable,

predictable projection

to propel me with prudence to my

predestined path and

prevent previous problems

from becoming precursors to a

premeditative presage.

Pretty protective purple pansies of

the four-leaf clover

from this lovely Amethyst Valley,
please lend me the four-leaf clover
which will protect and lead me out of
this lavender land and
do not prolong this promenade."

Knip Tibbar handed Old Wolf the chant which was embossed on a pink handkerchief.

"Oh, Mr. Tibbar! How in the world do you expect me to remember all those words? Even if they are written down for me, I cannot read!" lamented the Old Wolf.

"You are a foolish Old Wolf! You go around teaching Jack the power of believing and you have not learned your own lessons! Close your eyes to eliminate all the visual interference. That way your brain will not overload and it will be able to focus on the auditory channels. I will repeat the chant several times. The ticking of the clock will transport the words to the past, thus locking them in your brain. Before doing that, the most important thing is that you must believe that your brain will remember what is being taught. The rest is repetition, my friend, REPETITION!" exclaimed Mr. Tibbar in a staunch and commanding voice.

The Old Wolf closed his eyes and Mr. Knip Tibbar started repeating the pansies' chant as he held the pocket watch close to the wolf's ear. Old Wolf took a deep breath, closed his eyes, and listened to the words over and over. Little by little, the words began to merge with the ticking of the watch. A wide self-satisfied grin emerged on Old Wolf's lips, signaling that he had memorized all the words.

Knip Tibbar shook the Old Wolf who looked as though he had been hypnotized. Knip Tibbar told him to hurry across the lavender field before he would succumb to the never-ending restful sleep. Just as Knip Tibbar was about to embrace the Old Wolf, he gave another warning, "When you get on a ship, beware of lullabies sung by enchanting mermaids, as they will try to detour you from the path toward your destination. You will be fooled into thinking that you can dive under the sea for several minutes. Then, as you become mesmerized by the beauty of the oceanic world, you will forget that your lungs have run out of air. Panic will set in too late and you will become a victim of your own curiosity! You must remember to keep the four-leaf clover with you at all times until you return from the coast of Tuscany in the beautiful country of Italy where you will find Gepetto. You will be able to see the map on your GPS watch. Just remember that Italy is the country that looks like a knee-high boot. Be on the lookout for an unexpected, lovely surprise before you leave the Tuscan land. This surprise will bring much joy into your life."

The Old Wolf got up, feeling a bit groggy. He appeared to have missed the last part of Knip Tibbar's message. Old Wolf was feeling overjoyed and confident about having memorized the chant. The words kept repeating automatically inside his head as if his brain had been programmed. He could not make the words stop!

Old Wolf thanked Knip Tibbar for his patience, information, and great advice. He got his pocket watch back and said goodbye. He remembered to put the mirror and his pocket watch in separate pockets. He looked down at the Amethyst Valley and spotted the patch of purple pansies smack in the middle of the lavender flowers.

Old Wolf managed to get down to the valley and, he noticed how the dainty, timid, little flowers had beautiful eyes with long eyelashes and tiny yellow mouths. He greeted the purple pansies and without hesitation began to recite the chant word-by-word, just as Mr. Knip Tibbar had taught him.

All of a sudden, every single purple pansy turned around in surprise to look at Old Wolf as if the early sun had made its morning call. They let out a deep fragrant sigh and in unison all swayed their heads away from the center, uncovering the four- leaf clover. Old Wolf tip-toed to get closer and gently picked the four-leaf clover making sure he did not step on any of the purple pansies.

Then, he heard them chant a message to him as if the words were coming from an angelical choir:

"Keep the four-leaf clover

under your lapel

to keep you focused on the present

and protect you from problems.

It is our precious present

To keep you safe

on your present errand.

Do not present the four-leaf clover unless you need to prevent risky predicaments."

The Old Wolf thanked the purple pansies with the utmost cordiality and gently pinned the four-leaf clover under his lapel. He told them that he would remember their advice and promised to never abuse the power of the four-leaf clover. The pansies indeed looked enchanting and Old Wolf knew it was time to hurry out of the valley. With heartfelt gratitude, he bowed to them and quickly pranced toward a hill, trying to find the main path.

For a moment, Old Wolf stopped to program his GPS watch. He realized that he would have to cross a hill before reaching the seaport. Unfortunately, he began to feel his allergies, and an asthma attack starting. The pollen from all the flowers was making his nose and eyes itch and his breathing passages were beginning to constrict. Wheezing, sneezing, and gasping for air, he was running through Amethyst Valley to get to the hilltop where he could look down to find the shortest path to the seaport. Suddenly, he felt as though someone had tripped him and he tumbled back down toward the lavender field.

Out of nowhere, he heard a strange voice saying, "Not so fast, not so fast! Where do you think you are going with my Irish luck! I have been looking all over for the four-leaf clover and never realized those silly pansies were hiding it!" The voice was that of a leprechaun and Old Wolf watched with disbelief as the leprechaun snatched the four-leaf clover from under his lapel.

The Old Wolf could not believe his eyes! A leprechaun in Italy! This little unpleasant fellow was reminding him of Mr. Troll. He had to think of something fast or he would be doomed.

Nearby was one of the leprechaun's boots which had come off when he had tripped the wolf. Old Wolf grabbed the boot before the leprechaun could snatch it. "Now I have my bargaining tool!" thought Old Wolf to himself. "Oh, Mr. Leprechaun, if you are indeed an Irish leprechaun in a foreign land, you must have surely heard that every footstep is slow on an unknown path. But the man with the boot does not mind where he places his foot. Fame is more lasting than life and he who conquers himself, conquers an enemy. How good can luck be, if luck cannot be shared? You can choose to be greedy or you can choose to be nice by conquering your greed. If you do not give me the four-leaf clover, I will never get out of this valley. If I do not give you your boot, neither will you! Do you remember that the symbols of the four leaves in the clover are hope, faith, love, and luck? Please be sensible, honor the symbol, and let's make a fair trade before it's too late!" said the Old Wolf in a convincing tone.

The leprechaun knew he would be doomed without his boot, so he had no choice but to make the trade. In a grumpy voice, he replied, "Fear is worse than fighting and I do not wish to fear or fight you! Give me back my boot and you can have the four-leaf clover!"

The Old Wolf quickly made the trade and thanked the leprechaun for his wise decision saying, "A friend's eye is a good looking glass! Consider me a friend, not a foe!" They shook hands and each went his separate way out of the lavender field.

As soon as Old Wolf reached the seaport, he decided to run to the shoreline to soak his nose and wash his face. The salty sea water made his eyes and nose sting. However, a little discomfort was worth the relief from his allergies and asthma attack. Feeling much better, he headed toward the busy seaport. It was a bustling and overwhelming place for a countryside wolf.

He decided to inquire about the ships headed for the Coast of Tuscany. He found a tourist ship ready to embark. The name of the ship was *Fortunato* and it was loaded with anxious and noisy tourists eager to visit Tuscany for the Chianti Wine Festival. Old Wolf scurried toward the ship, pushing his way through the crowded seaport until he managed to locate

Captain Mario. The captain was a bold, young looking fellow with several long braids pinned back in a pony tail. He had a mean looking French bulldog named Brutus by his side and a talking blue parrot named Bambolino sitting on top of his shoulder. Old Wolf managed to make a bargain with the captain to clean the deck in exchange for a small cabin and a daily meal.

Captain Mario was a man of few words, but he firmly warned Old Wolf, "Just be sure to remember that no one ever dares do anything wrong aboard the *Fortunato*, or I will command Brutus to terrorize him with his frightening growl which usually makes him jump overboard never to be seen or heard from again! I also do not engage in conversations!

I am Captain Mario and I must concentrate on keeping the ship on course. I pay attention to my parrot Bambolino because he keeps me informed about the force of the winds and the approaching storms! Make sure you keep away from Bambolino and do not think of him as your next bird meal or your talking pal! Do we understand each other clearly, Mr. Old Wolf? If it is so, we have a deal!"

Stunned by Captain Mario's remarks, Old Wolf proceeded to reply, "My Captain, your orders are clearly understood! I am a vegetarian wolf and I would never consider Bambolino a meal! As a matter of fact, my best friend is the Little Red Hen. I promise not to be a problem for anyone and I will keep your ship's deck shiny day and night."

Captain Mario had heard enough. He commanded one of his sailors to show Old Wolf to his small cabin where he was given a bucket, scrub brush, and mop.

Soon the *Fortunato* was ready to depart. The large, massive, white sails were hoisted and all the passengers waved goodbye to the cheering crowd wishing them a bon voyage. The mood was joyful and expectations were high. Old Wolf kept busy cleaning the deck and trying to stay balanced as the ship sailed through the rough waves. The passengers were friendly, cheerful, and polite, but they certainly kept Old Wolf busy mopping and scrubbing their spills.

As darkness swallowed the daylight on the fifth night, poor Old Wolf discovered the true meaning of "seasickness." The winds grew fierce and the *Fortunato* rode each and every wave as a surfing champion. All the passengers were ordered to go below deck and stay in their cabins. The only ones remaining on deck were Captain Mario with Bambolino clinging to his braids, Brutus howling at the wind, and the sailors who were lowering the sails. Old Wolf hung onto the railing and to what was left of his guts. Dizzy and disoriented, he found the nearest lounge chair that was chained to the deck. Old Wolf managed to squeeze himself between a loose horizontal strap of a deck chair and use it as a safety belt while waiting for the storm to subside. Later that day, as dusk turned to night and night turned to dawn, the winds calmed and the storm passed. The sound of seagulls and pelicans never sounded so melodically refreshing and welcoming.

Feeling exhausted from riding the rough sea, Old Wolf decided to take a nap on the deck chair. Soon after that, a distant soothing lullaby sung by the most incredible voices reached his ears. The Old Wolf remembered the warning that Knip Tibbar had given him about the mermaids.

Old Wolf checked under his lapel to make sure the four-leaf clover was still pinned there. He cautiously approached the railing to glance at the horizon. To his disbelief, he saw the sea full of beautiful mermaids beckoning him to go for a swim. He quickly pulled out the mirror and the pocket watch and, as if violently thrown from past to future, he came back to his senses to focus on his present task. The sound of the lullabies faded and the mermaids disappeared in the wink of an eye. The Old Wolf staggered back from the railing, wondering if he had been dreaming or if the vision of the mermaids had been real.

Early that morning he heard a sailor shout aloud, "Land ahoy!" The Tuscan Coast was in clear sight and Old Wolf was overjoyed as he prepared to disembark. He programmed Gepetto's address into his GPS watch. Before leaving the ship, he found Captain Mario to personally thank him for the opportunity to sail aboard his ship.

Captain Mario seemed to be in a cheerful mood and gave Old Wolf a jolly strong slap on the back which almost knocked the breath out of him. Captain Mario told him, "You are welcome aboard my ship anytime!"

Bambolino, perched firmly on Captain Mario's shoulder, kept repeating, *"Ciao bambinos, ciao bambinas, in bocca al lupo!"* Meanwhile, Brutus kept busy deciding whether to chew his bone or scratch his fleas.

As Old Wolf stepped off the gangplank, the young Italian boys and girls spied Bambolino on his shoulder and cried out *"Crepi, crepi! Ciao Bambolino!"*

Old Wolf curiously asked a bystander "What are they saying?"

The bystander took one long look at the wolf and hesitated before answering, "The literal translation is '*Good-bye boys, good-bye girls, in the mouth of the wolf!*' And they are answering '*Death, death!*'" Realizing the wolf was about to faint, she assured him by saying, "Don't worry wolf! It is a common Italian idiom to wish people good luck and it means no harm to wolves. It is the equivalent of the English saying, '*Break a leg!*'"

Old Wolf did not attempt to understand the Italian or English idioms. Both of them made him uncomfortable. Old Wolf did not want to waste any time getting to the village. He had to choose between hiring a horse-drawn wagon or a scooter-taxi. Feeling secure and unruffled, he chose the horse-drawn wagon to better appreciate the beautiful landscape tapestry of the Tuscan countryside.

Old Wolf showed an old Italian driver the map on his GPS watch. The driver acknowledged being familiar with the famous woodworker's shop. They agreed on a reasonable fare and were on their way to find Gepetto.

As they rode through the meadow Old Wolf felt as though he had been surrounded by a breathtaking patchwork of autumn colors. As the wagon rolled down to the small town, the driver sang cheerful Italian melodies, and the horse kept a steady pace until they reached Gepetto's front door.

It was hard for Old Wolf to believe he had finally reached his destination. He paid the fare for the ride and patted the horse in gratitude. Then he proceeded on the cobblestone sidewalk to the wooden door where he raised and dropped the metal knocker several times. He peeked through the window where he could see old Gepetto shuffling slowly toward the door.

At first, Gepetto explained that it was late and he was no longer open for business.

Old Wolf introduced himself and told Gepetto that he had traveled a long distance because he wanted to help Gepetto rescue Pinocchio.

Gepetto could not comprehend why a total stranger would want to come to his aid. He was touched by this stranger's kind act and began to explain, "You see, Old Wolf , the last time I rescued my dear Pinocchio, I endured many hardships. I was so pleased when he promised to never tell a lie again. Unfortunately, even after the Blue Fairy turned him into a real boy, Pinocchio broke his promise. Once more, he ran away from school to return to Toyland. This time the police found him and the courts sent him to a boarding school, where children are not allowed to leave until they learn to read, write, and memorize the times tables. Pinocchio is a bit hard-headed, and his brain does not learn very fast, even though he was made from a fine piece of pine wood. I am afraid I will be too old by the time Pinocchio passes his exit exam and is allowed to come home!"

The Old Wolf had a grand idea! He would figure out how he could get into the boarding school and, once there, find a way to help Pinocchio pass the exit exam. It would be somewhat challenging because he also would have to learn the same subjects to be able to get out.

Gepetto sighed and said, "Mr. Old Wolf, the law in this land is very strict and it doesn't matter how old you are or where you come from, you must be literate or they will put you in a boarding school.

Old Wolf smiled and replied, "In that case, I will be the perfect candidate to get Pinocchio out! You see, I am as illiterate as can be! For many years I have wanted to learn how to read and write! Now I have the perfect opportunity to do so. At the same time, I will have a chance to rescue Pinocchio, once and for all! This will be my last venture and challenge before I return to Green Valley to buy a piece of land from Little Red Hen. I want to live the rest of my years close to my dear friends."

Gepetto was perplexed, worried, and indecisive about such a risky undertaking. He replied, "Oh, Mr. Old Wolf, you have a daring and caring heart! It is unheard of, especially coming from a lone wolf. If you feel so strongly about it, then let your heart and good common sense decide. I guess this would provide you with a good opportunity to kill two birds with one stone."

Old Wolf looked at Gepetto in disbelief and with an anguished tone replied, "What is this business about killing two birds with one stone? I am a vegetarian wolf who would never, ever think of hurting or killing any birds, chickens, or parrots! Why do others always assume that I would do such awful things? I only want to rescue Pinocchio and learn how to read and write!

Gepetto smiled and apologized for upsetting the wolf. "It is only an idiom which means that you will get two tasks done at the same time. No pun intended. On the contrary, of course, if the plan works for both of you, I will be the happiest man on earth!"

Old Wolf was relieved and delighted and said, "Let us not waste any time! Call the police and turn me in. Tell them that you found an illiterate wolf trying to do business transactions without being able to sign his own name! Go on, Gepetto, make the call!"

Gepetto phoned the police with mixed feelings of trepidation and joy. Two policemen arrived promptly at his door. They arrested the Old Wolf for not being able to show proof that he could sign his name to match the signature on his passport. Old Wolf wrote an "X" when they asked him to sign his name which convinced the policemen that he was an illiterate wolf. The next day, the court decided to send him straight to the boarding school, instead of jail.

Within the hour, Old Wolf found himself at the boarding school. He tried to pretend that he was worried, but deep inside, he was so happy to have reached his final destination where his plan to rescue Pinocchio would begin to unfold. He looked everywhere until he spotted poor Pinocchio who had been reverted into his marionette form. Even more distressing, he had grown long ears and a donkey's tail. Then Old Wolf thought to himself, "At least, I was already born with long ears and a tail. I just hope I don't lose them after I learn to read and write! I remember how badly it hurt when my tail got burned at the Three Little Pigs' house!"

It was not until recess when Old Wolf had an opportunity to introduce himself to Pinocchio and tell him about his plan. Pinocchio previously had been fooled by a fox and a cat so he was not too eager to trust a strange wolf unless he could show him some proof. Old Wolf took out the watch and instantly a yo-yo with Pinocchio's face carved on its side emerged. Pinocchio recognized it right away! There was no longer a doubt in his mind that the plan was real and he began to sob profusely.

The playground supervisor heard the commotion and demanded to know what had happened. The Old Wolf lied by pretending he had pushed Pinocchio. After all, he was not about to reveal the plan. The supervisor immediately punished the wolf for making Pinocchio cry. He pulled Old Wolf by one of his ears and told him to stand in the hot sun in the middle of the courtyard for half an hour. He also warned Old Wolf that if he disobeyed the rules again, the punishment would be more severe the next time.

The days came and the days went. The Old Wolf and Pinocchio spent long hours trying to learn how to read and write Italian and English. Both of them mastered reading and writing Italian without too much trouble. However, they were very confused when it came to learning English.

Neither of them could learn to decode or spell. Pinocchio kept complaining and crying every day saying, "Why do I have to learn English? English vowels don't make any sense! When I say *'you'*; I do not hear the /o/! When I say *'your'*; I do not hear the /u/! When I say 'one'; the 'o' sounds like a /wa/! When I say '*women*'; the 'o' sounds like an /i/! English vowels are crazy! How about all the silent letters in so many words! And then, you have some consonants and digraphs which have different pronunciations! How can I ever learn to read or spell English correctly? How will I ever pass the exit exam? I'll never be able get out of this place!"

Old Wolf felt the same way, but did not say so because he did not want Pinocchio to get discouraged. He decided that it was best to let Pinocchio know about Gepetto's plans. "Pinocchio, you have to stop complaining. You have to learn English because when you get out, Gepetto is taking you to America. He is getting too old to take care of you. The Blue Fairy found a job for you in a famous amusement park where you will be able to live and work the rest of your life! Gepetto will be allowed to stay with you. Think about it, a miracle! Pinocchio, they say it is better than Toyland! They will give you a special place and pay you to entertain children and adults! How lucky can you be? But first, you must learn to read and write English! Tomorrow they are sending us to the special school on top of the hill where they will teach us to read and write English using *Ellie's Code*."

Pinocchio's mood changed as soon as he heard the plans about going to live in an amusement park. With great enthusiasm and curiosity he asked, "How long will it take us to learn *Ellie's Code*? When is Gepetto going to pick me up? How long is the trip to America? "

The Old Wolf answered, "I have heard the color code is simple, Pinocchio. We don't have to memorize the Code, we simply learn to use it to guide us to decode words and become better English spellers. One step at a time, Pinocchio! Go to bed and get ready to work hard every day so we can get out of here. I don't want to hear you cry or complain, anymore!" Quickly Pinocchio went to sleep with a smile on his face.

After eight weeks of instruction, Pinocchio and the Old Wolf were finally able to read and write Italian **AND** English!

The only remaining problem was that they could not memorize all the times tables! The day of the final exam was fast approaching and Old Wolf had to think of a solution to this dilemma or both of them would be stuck at the boarding school for another six months! Their small dorm room was wallpapered with the times tables flash cards. They took turns trying to memorize them by chanting, but it was absolutely no use! They kept getting confused and forgetting the answers. Old Wolf looked at Pinocchio in quiet desperation and, after hours of exhausting practice, both fell asleep.

As Old Wolf fell into a deep sleep, he started to dream. He heard Knip Tibbar's voice scolding him, "Learn your own lessons, Old Wolf! Let the four-leaf clover guide you to find a solution to the times tables. Use the pocket watch to lock up the strategies in your mind. The answers are in the patterns! The answers are in the PATTERNS! Believe that it can be done!"

Old Wolf woke up startled and looked around to see if Mr. Knip Tibbar could actually be hiding somewhere in the small room. The dream appeared to be real! He tried to make sense of it and placed the four-leaf clover on top of his desk. He took out the mirror and wished he could take a peek at the day of the final exam. The mirror started flashing many images as if it was fast-forwarding pictures into the future. When it stopped, there was a clear episode where Old Wolf could see Pinocchio sitting in the front row and saw himself seated in the back of the classroom. They were busy writing an essay and when finished, one by one, each student was asked to go in front of the class to read some pages from a book. Both did splendid on this part of the language arts exam! Then, every student had to pick a number from a box. Strictly by chance, each student had to prove that he knew his times tables by correctly multiplying the number he had chosen. Pinocchio drew the number nine from the box. He was asked to multiply one through ten by nines. Old Wolf drew the number five and was asked to multiply by fives. However, after the teacher looked at Old Wolf, she gave him a more difficult problem because he was an older student. She asked him to multiply a five digit figure by five! At this very moment, Pinocchio woke up and interrupted the revelation of the mirror. The image faded and Old Wolf had to put the mirror back in his pocket. He told Pinocchio about the dream and tried to make him feel better by telling him that he would have to focus on learning the nines while he had to learn the fives.

Instead of being happy, Pinocchio started crying and whining, "That is not fair! The fives are easier and I will get the more difficult nines!"

Once again, Old Wolf had to tell Pinocchio to stop crying and complaining and go back to sleep. He, meanwhile, was going to stay up all night to figure out the patterns. It did not take long to convince Pinocchio to go back to sleep. After tucking Pinocchio in bed, Old Wolf stared at the four-leaf clover, wishing he could spot the multiplication patterns. He looked at the answers to the times tables for the nines trying to find patterns he could identify. After staring at the questions and the answers for a very long time, his mind became tired, his eyes drooped and, before long, Old Wolf was sound asleep.

Old Wolf began to dream again. He could see Mr. Knip Tibbar dancing with a pretty lady bunny chanting the clue to the nines to the rhythm of a song that sounded similar to *The Farmer in the Dell*:

Descending order for the **1**s

Ascending order for the **10**s

Both digits in the answer

Always add up to **9**

When you begin to multiply **9** by **6**

All partners switch around!

You start by asking what number comes
before the one you are asked
to multiply by **9**.

Place that partial answer
on the column of the **10**s
and figure out its partner
which adds up to **9**.

Place that one in the column of the **1**s
then read the two digits together
to give you what you want!

The **9** dances alone
when multiplied by **1**

He partners with the **0**
When multiplied by **10**

Either way its digits

still add up to **9**

The **1** dances with the **8**

or the **8** dances with the **1**

Together tap and clap

18 or **81**

The **2** joins elbows with the **7**

and **7** joins elbows with the **2**

Together tap and clap

27 or **72**

The **3** must find the **6**

and the **6** must find the **3**

Together tap and clap

36 or **63**

The **4** and **5** are always next to each

    other in front or behind

    only the question makes that matter!

Together tap and clap

    a **45** or **54**

Patterns my dear

    patterns are here

    patterns are there

    patterns, patterns, patterns

    patterns are everywhere!

He woke up startled and fumbled for a paper and pencil. He scribbled some quick calculations to make sure the chant made sense and provided the right answers. It did! It all became so clear and easy! Old Wolf came to the realization that by using this pattern Pinocchio would also learn the nines in a very short time. Old Wolf kept repeating the chant as he joyfully danced around the room.

Once he knew how to get the answers to the nines, Old Wolf was more excited to start working on the fives. A strange thing happened when he was staring at the numbers of an old clock. It was as though the answers were jumping out of the old clock and he could hear the voice of Mr. Knip Tibbar once more:

All the even numbers multiplied by **5**
end in a **0**

All the odd numbers multiplied by **5,**
end in a **5**.

Look at each digit you are multiplying
by **5**
and divide it by half.

Write it down

and multiply that half by **10**

You simply add a **0**

for the even numbers.

Or move the decimal point to the right

for the odd ones!

That is what the long hand of the watch

does when it gets on the **6**

To read the minutes

it divides the **6** in half

which is **3**

And then just adds the **0**

to say **30!**

When it gets on the **9**

45 minutes have passed

Because half of **9**

Is **4.5!**

All you do

is remove the decimal point!

And that is how the clock

gives you the multiplication

answers to the **5s**

as it reads the minute intervals

5 by **5!**

Old Wolf had never felt so smart in his whole life! He was so sure of himself! He knew it would be possible to calculate faster than anyone, even if they used a calculator! Before going to bed, he carefully placed the four-leaf clover behind his lapel. He couldn't wait to teach Pinocchio!

The next day Old Wolf and Pinocchio spent the whole day dancing to the tune of the nines and dividing numbers by half to get the answers to the fives. There was no doubt in their minds that they would be able to pass the test. They actually had fun learning the times tables!

One by one, they found patterns to each of the multiplication tables. It no longer mattered which times tables they would be asked to multiply. They had learned all of the times tables!

The day of the exam came. Old Wolf and Pinocchio were ready. Pinocchio had one of the highest scores and Old Wolf earned a medal for beating the teacher who could not multiply a five-digit number by five as fast as the wolf, even with a calculator! Old Wolf was busy writing the answers while the teacher was still entering the problem! All the classmates cheered for Old Wolf and called him the "Multiplication Champion."

Gepetto was surprised and overjoyed when he received an official letter from the boarding school notifying him that Pinocchio had passed his exit exams and would be allowed to go home. An invitation to his graduation was enclosed with the letter. Gepetto packed a small suitcase with his best suit for the special occasion. He waited anxiously for the special day when he would be able to see Pinocchio walk across the graduation stage to receive his diploma. He would then take his son to America to establish a new home. This meant that his marionette son was finally literate and that was cause for a great celebration.

Graduation day was one of Old Wolf and Pinocchio's best days ever! Pinocchio's ears had shrunk and his tail had completely disappeared. Gepetto was overcome with joy to see and hug Pinocchio, once again. He felt so proud that his marionette son was finally able to read, write, and multiply.

Old Wolf was ecstatic to be able to read and write on his own. He could hardly wait to send text messages to all of his friends.

When Old Wolf saw Gepetto packing Pinocchio's clothes, he was overcome with a mixture of pride, happiness, and a sense of accomplishment. He knew his task was done and it was time to leave. He would return to Green Valley where he would see the Little Red Hen.

Gepetto hugged Old Wolf and said, "I am so grateful for what you have done for my son. Thanks to you, I finally have my dear Pinocchio back! The Blue Fairy said she would turn him into a real boy when she can be sure that he has a conscience. I brought all of our packed belongings in a wagon. After the graduation ceremony, we plan to go straight to the harbor. Please allow us to give you a ride."

Old Wolf was happy to join them for the long ride. First, they went back to thank their teachers and say good-bye to their friends. Soon after, the three were on their way to the seaport. The mood was joyful. All three sang Italian songs as they rode through the beautiful countryside.

It was around noon when they decided to take a short detour to rest along the side of a dirt road. The road was bumpy and one of the wheels broke. Gepetto and the Old Wolf unloaded the wagon to repair the wheel. The Old Wolf got under the wagon to loosen the screws. To his surprise, he caught a glimpse of a beautiful female gypsy silver wolf walking down the same path, followed by her three cute cubs. She was carrying a heavy load on her back while her cubs ran happily all over the place. Old Wolf did not hesitate and with a flirty tone he asked, "Where are you headed with that heavy load, wolfelina bella?"

"My goodness, gracious! I almost did not see you, wolf! Let me introduce myself. My name is Hope, and these are my cubs: This is Faith, that one over there is Luck, and my youngest is Love. We are pleased to meet you. We are gypsy wolves and we are on our way to the seaport," Hope replied in a sweet voice.

Old Wolf's ears reverberated with the familiar sound of the names Faith, Hope, Luck, and Love. It was as if he had heard them before. Soon after, he realized the coincidence as he gently patted the four-leaf clover and remembered the last message that Mr. Knip Tibbar had given him. "Mr. Knip Tibbar, you are indeed a shrewd soothsayer and the best matchmaker in the whole world! Now I remember the last part of your message! I hope these four wolves will become my true four-leaf clover from now on! All four gypsy wolves: I hope to call you my own true family one day soon!" he whispered to himself as he offered them a ride.

"If you are so kind as to offer us a ride, we will be obliged to take it. My load is quite heavy and the seaport is still far away," responded Hope in an enchanting voice.

Old Wolf was struck by Hope's beauty and could not keep his eyes off her. He did not waste any time offering his help to remove the load off her back.

The cubs immediately started playing with Pinocchio. They ran around chasing each other playing tag.

Gepetto took his tool box from the wagon and placed it near the wheel. He was amused as he watched the love-struck Old Wolf trying to fix the wheel while keeping his eyes on Hope. Old Wolf hammered his paw, instead of the nail, and pretended it did not hurt. Gepetto told him he could handle the wheel repairs and dismissed the wolf, freeing him to talk to Hope while keeping an eye on Pinocchio and the cubs.

Soon after, they were back on the road headed to the seaport. This was the happiest ride for the Old Wolf and he actually wished it would never end. Old Wolf told Hope about his adventures and Hope kept them entertained all the way to the seaport by singing gypsy songs. They reached the busy seaport. Old Wolf had managed to persuade Hope to return with him to the Green Valley. He did not waste any time and sent a text message to Captain Mario to find out if he could make reservations for seven, instead of one! He also convinced Gepetto to spend some time in Green Valley while he and Pinocchio waited for the ship which would take them to America.

The reply from Captain Mario came quickly! "You are a crazy Old Wolf! You are lucky that in Italy we say the more the merrier! I am a man of my word. You and your pack will be welcomed aboard the *Fortunato* anytime!"

As soon as they approached the dock, Old Wolf could hear Bambolino's welcoming screams a mile away. *"Benvenuto bambinos, benvenuto bambinas!"* he kept repeating as the passengers boarded the ship.

Old Wolf spotted Captain Mario. He hurried to greet him and introduce his friends, especially his sweetheart lady wolf.

In a jolly mood, Captain Mario extended a warm welcome to the wolf and his pack by saying, "It is good to see you again, Old Wolf! I am glad to meet all of you! You are welcome to board my ship. I am sure I can find a chore for each and every one of you! Life is beautiful, but we must all earn our keep in this world. Old Wolf, since I heard that you are now a very literate wolf, you will be in charge of helping the passengers send emails to their loved ones. Lady Hope, I heard you can sing beautiful gypsy songs! You can sing for the passengers at dinner time. Gepetto, you are a skilled craftsman! I will ask you to help with repairs when necessary. Pinocchio, you will be my messenger. Faith, Luck, and Love, all three of you will be in charge of the lost and found. I know you like to run around, so you can help by bringing back any items you find left behind by the passengers."

This was going to be Pinocchio's last trip before he and Gepetto would transfer to a transatlantic ship bound for America. For some reason, they both kept asking if the captain had seen any whales in the ocean. He kept replying that he had seen only sharks.

This time, Captain Mario treated the Old Wolf and his companions to a fancier and more comfortable cabin. They stowed their belongings in their accommodations. Fortunately, Pinocchio, Luck, Faith, and Love did not mind having to share a bunk bed.

Pinocchio was very curious about everything that Captain Mario said or did. The captain did not seem to mind the inquisitive mind of the little one.

Pinocchio challenged the cubs to play hide and go seek. He ran all over the deck trying to find a place to hide until he found the captain's cabin door slightly ajar. He hurried inside and was startled when he ran right into Captain Mario who lifted him in the air and said, "Pinocchio, Pinocchio I have heard all about you and you remind me of myself! I will share a secret with you! I was born a marionette, also! Everyone in town pulled on my strings and I did not have the common sense to understand how my actions and lies were wrong or caused grief to others. I took so many risks until one day I fell off a ship and a great white shark swallowed me whole! I had to survive inside his crowded, dark, slimy guts for over a week eating nothing but fish! I was lucky because the shark could not digest my marionette's pinewood body. Otherwise, I would have become another casualty of his digestive system! I managed to tickle his stomach until he had no choice but to throw me up. I found myself back on the ocean, floating.

The Blue Fairy picked me up from the floating debris and gave me one last chance. She told me that she could turn me into a real man only if I would develop a conscience. Of course, I promised to do whatever she suggested. Then she cut my strings like freeing me from my own net, transformed my wooden body to real flesh, except for one wooden leg which I still hide inside my boot. She told me that my wooden leg would be a reminder of my promise to never forget to use my conscience. She gave me this ship and shortened my name to Mario.

Since that unforgettable day, no one has ever called me a marionette or has needed to tell me what to do! Now, everyone treats me with respect because I am Captain Mario and I command the seas better than any captain in these waters! My ship's name is the *Fortunato*. It is an appropriate name for the ship, because, thanks to that second opportunity the Blue Fairy gave me, I have become a very fortunate man! Don't mess up your chances, Pinocchio! You never know when it may be the last one!"

Pinocchio was so impressed! He decided to be just like Captain Mario! He told him, "You are my hero! When the Blue Fairy takes me to the amusement park, I am going to become the main attraction! I will ask her to build a ship like the *Fortunato* so I can pretend to be just like you, Captain Mario! I owe everything to Gepetto for risking his life to rescue me! I also owe the Old Wolf because, without him, I would still be locked up at the boarding school unable to read, write, or multiply. I promise to be good! I will never tell a lie again!"

Captain Mario put him down, gave him his compass and said, "Take this gift as a souvenir, Pinocchio! My compass will remind you to think where your actions will take you before deciding which course to take! Don't ever let me find out that you have lied again!

You don't want to find out what will happen! Now move along and let's get this voyage started!"

Pinocchio felt so privileged to have Captain Mario's compass! He shook his hand, saluted the captain, and said, "Thanks a million, Captain Mario! I promise never to lie or cause trouble, again!" While still awestruck, Pinocchio hurried out of the cabin to find Gepetto and show him the compass which he proudly displayed. Suddenly, Pinocchio heard the cubs calling out his name.

"There you are, Pinocchio! Where have you been hiding? We have been looking all over the ship for you!" all three cubs shouted as they ran towards him.

Gepetto, who had been keeping a close eye on Pinocchio, had overheard the whole conversation. He had been hiding behind Captain Mario's cabin door as Pinocchio darted out to find him. Gepetto was feeling relieved thinking that this time Pinocchio would keep his word.

Captain Mario came out of his cabin and bumped into Gepetto. "I know his type better than anyone! He should not trouble you, anymore!" the captain exclaimed in a confident voice.

Gepetto replied, "Thank you for your words of advice, Captain. Pinocchio really looks up to you. Your influence and advice have made a great impact on him."

Captain Mario winked and gave a thumbs up. He proceeded to put Bambolino on his shoulder and secured Brutus' leash before he gave a loud command to his crew, "It is time to get this ship sailing! Everyone to his post!" One could feel the excitement as the sailors started climbing the masts to raise the sails. A gust of wind got the ship moving as the passengers cheered and waved good-bye to the seaport crowd. Soon the Tuscan coast was in the distance and finally it faded out of sight.

The sea was calm and the *Fortunato* kept a steady course. Old Wolf kept busy sending emails for the tourists. He also sent emails to all of his friends. What a delight it was to feel confident in his ability to read and write. He finally understood the power of communication! He kept thinking about all the books he would be able to read and the stories he could read to the cubs. With Hope and the cubs by his side, he would never feel lonely again.

Lady Hope enchanted the tourists with her captivating gypsy songs. She became the main attraction during dinner time. The tourists were eager to take pictures with her and get her autograph.

Pinocchio turned out to be a very efficient and responsible messenger boy. He felt important and privileged to be in charge of bringing messages to Captain Mario.

The cubs kept busy looking for lost items. In a short time, they became good detectives by sniffing the items and figuring out which lost item belonged to each passenger.

Gepetto proved to be a fine and handy craftsman. He kept busy repairing the sails and broken furniture on the ship.

As the days came and went, it was clear to everyone that the Old Wolf and Hope had become an inseparable and perfect couple.

The *Fortunato* finally arrived at Green Valley seaport. Old Wolf borrowed Captain Mario's binoculars to see if Mr. Knip Tibbar had come to pick them up as promised in one of his emails. It took no time at all to spot his pink rabbit ears sticking out of his top hat! Old Wolf was relieved to know that his friend was waiting for them!

Captain Mario reminded his crew, "You have a week to rest and relax before you must return to the ship. The *Fortunato* will sail with or without you!" Then, he placed Bambolino on his shoulder and told Brutus to start walking. With that, they joined Old Wolf on shore. They were going to spend the entire week of shore leave with Old Wolf and his family!

Old Wolf was so happy to introduce his new family and friends to Mr. Knip Tibbar who smiled and greeted them as if he had already known them.

Mr. Knip Tibbar exclaimed, "There is a very pleasant surprise waiting for you at the other end of this valley. We must quickly get going because we need to cross Amethyst Valley before noon to return the four-leaf clover to the pansies. The fragrance of the lavender field gets more pungent in the afternoon and we must not keep friends waiting."

They rode in Knip Tibbar's grand old carriage. When they reached the top of the plateau, they could see the beautiful lavender field and the patch of purple pansies.

Bambolino kept repeating, "Pretty flowers, pretty flowers!"

Brutus fell asleep on Captain Mario's lap. He was not used to riding in a horse-drawn carriage.

Mr. Knip Tibbar warned Captain Mario that when they got close to the pansy patch, Bambolino would have to stay quiet and that everyone else stay in the carriage."

When they arrived at the pansy patch, Captain Mario put a bandana over Bambolino's head to keep him quiet. It was useless! Bambolino kept repeating, "It's dark in here, it's dark in here!" until Captain Mario was forced to hold his beak shut to keep him quiet.

Mr. Knip Tibbar said, "Old Wolf, please hold the four-leaf clover in your hand. Only the two of us will walk over to return it to the pansies. Everyone else has to stay in the carriage. You must all be very still and quiet!"

Mr. Knip Tibbar led the way to the pansies and Old Wolf followed. When they were close to them, Knip Tibbar took out his pocket watch and opened the back cover. A beautiful melody played and gold dust sprayed all over the pansy patch. The purple pansies sighed and retreated as Mr. Knip Tibbar gently placed the four-leaf clover in the middle of the patch. He said to them, "Pretty, precious, purple pansies, we have come to return the four-leaf clover. We thank you for sharing it to ensure the pleasing outcomes of this well deserving passenger of life. We trust that you will always keep this precious clover safe in this peaceful hideaway."

The purple pansies smiled and replied, "You are welcome, Mr. Tibbar. Our job is to be the keepers of time and to present the four-leaf clover to those who can create the most positive outcome at the present time."

Mr. Knip Tibbar and Old Wolf retreated to the carriage and sped away.

They knew they had to get out of the lavender field in a hurry because they were without the protection of the four-leaf clover. Time was of the essence.

Bambolino was upset when Captain Mario released his beak. He sounded grumpy repeating, "That was not nice! That was not nice!"

Old Wolf could not believe the sight when they approached the old cypress tree on top of the hill! Every one of his friends was lined up on the road to greet him! He jumped out of the carriage to hug each and every one of them.

First, he ran to hug his best
friend, the Little Red Hen, who had
traveled such a long way with her
three chicks, the cat, the dog, and the
duck! "We have missed you so much
since the day you left, Mr. Old Wolf!
It is so good to see you again!" They
each crowded around to give him a
hug. Little Red Hen presented him with
his favorite pizza and title to a parcel
of land on her farm.

Old Wolf hugged her and thanked her. "Little Red Hen, you have always been such a wonderful friend! I will gladly take the pizza, but I want to pay you for the land. I still plan to help you with the planting, harvesting, and carrying your wheat to the mill."

Old Wolf then rushed to the other side of the road to hug Jack and his mother, tell them how much he had missed them, and how happy he was to see them. They handed Old Wolf his favorite delicious green bean casserole. Next to them, the Warlock of Moss, the cat with the funny hat, Chicken Little, Mr. Troll, and a patched-up Humpty Dumpty waited eagerly to have a chance to hug an old friend!

Behind the tree were the Three Little Pigs, feeling shy and apologetic for having made the wrong assumption about the Old Wolf. "We wish to apologize for burning your tail, Mr. Old Wolf. We were afraid you were going to eat us! Our mama always told us to beware of strangers and never open the door," explained the Three Little Pigs.

"Don't worry about it, Little Pigs! I am glad you are no longer afraid of me. I still would like for us to be friends. You were right to obey your mother's advice," replied the Old Wolf.

Everyone was delighted to see the Old Wolf and meet his new family and friends. They had prepared a grand old picnic celebration to welcome back a dear friend.

Old Wolf didn't know if he should cry or smile with all the excitement. He couldn't help feeling so emotional about the whole thing. After all, he was still a sentimental wolf!

Then, Mr. Tibbar tapped on his glass to get everyone's attention and, with an authoritarian voice, began to make a toast: "Oh, Mr. Old Wolf, how good it is to see predictions come to be. We see you found your precious lady wolf along with her cubs to keep you company and provide you with a complete family. This was how your fate was predestined to be. Your prospect to rescue precocious Pinocchio was done with prowess and priceless precision! The Little Red Hen and Jack also have shared testimonies about your altruistic nature. Your lack of presumption, pretense, or desire to profit from your

actions, makes you praiseworthy! We proclaim you our true hero! This is a precious day for all who have had the privilege to know you and have come from yonder to this premier gathering to wish you a prodigious and propitious future! The presence of all your friends gathered here to make this special preparation is a testimony to the prevalent and profound sentiment which they proclaim, profess, and project towards you! Let the celebration begin and may this day be just the prelude to a plentitude of delightful and prosperous days!"

The celebration began. Old Wolf reveled in the joyful gathering of friends. They danced, sang, played games, and talked about old times. They were all eager to hear about the Old Wolf's adventures. He was a great storyteller. The gathering and celebration lasted several days.

When the celebration was over, Pinocchio and Gepetto continued their journey to America. Pinocchio became one of the main attractions at the amusement park. He never broke his promise and always kept in touch with Captain Mario who still sails his ship with Bambolino and Brutus. Pinocchio calls him his "second papa."

All the friends have promised to take a cruise together aboard the *Fortunato* once a year! Captain Mario enjoys taking his friends back to Tuscany. He is always accompanied by Bambolino, who remains as talkative as ever, and Brutus, who now wears a fancy flea collar.

Mr. Knip Tibbar spends every Easter and Christmas visiting the Old Wolf. They love to spend hours having long conversations.

Jack and his mother also visit the Old Wolf and his family. They always bring their best green beans for everyone's enjoyment. They are known as the green bean giants of the Green Valley. Every year Jack retells his story about how the Old Wolf helped him get his business started with seven magical green bean seeds!

The Warlock of Moss keeps updating everyone about the newest electrical gadgets he has personally designed.

The cubs have grown up and help around the farm. Each one is building his own house near the farm.

The chicks turned out to be one good-looking rooster and two young hens that look just like their mother. Little Red Hen invites the Old Wolf and his family for pizza every Saturday!

The Three Little Pigs all built strong brick houses and live close to the Old Wolf. They visit him and his family on weekends. They are learning how to become great farmers. They are good friends with the cubs and the chicks.

To this day, it is known that Old Wolf still lives on the land he purchased adjacent to Little Red Hen's farm. He often sits outside on his porch rocking in his chair, writing his

memoirs on a laptop computer, and reminding Hope about the three best days of his life: the day he met her on an old road in Tuscany; the day he and Pinocchio learned to read, write and multiply; and the day when all of his dear friends gathered to celebrate his return.

He is a very happy Old Wolf and has absolutely no regrets in life!

Made in the USA
Middletown, DE
09 July 2022

68881638R00055